GOD IN 3 PERSONS

Understanding the Trinity
John 1:1-3

SEASON

JOHN

In the beginning was the Word,
and the Word was with God,
and the Word was God.
He was in the beginning
with God.

1:1-3

New King
James Version

All things were made through Him, and without Him nothing was made that was made.

Hi, my name is Marlene. I just met the greatest person in my life! What I learned is so important that I'm telling everyone.

My friends and I will tell you all about it.

How many triangles do you see?

There is only 1 triangle. Similarly, there is only 1 God.

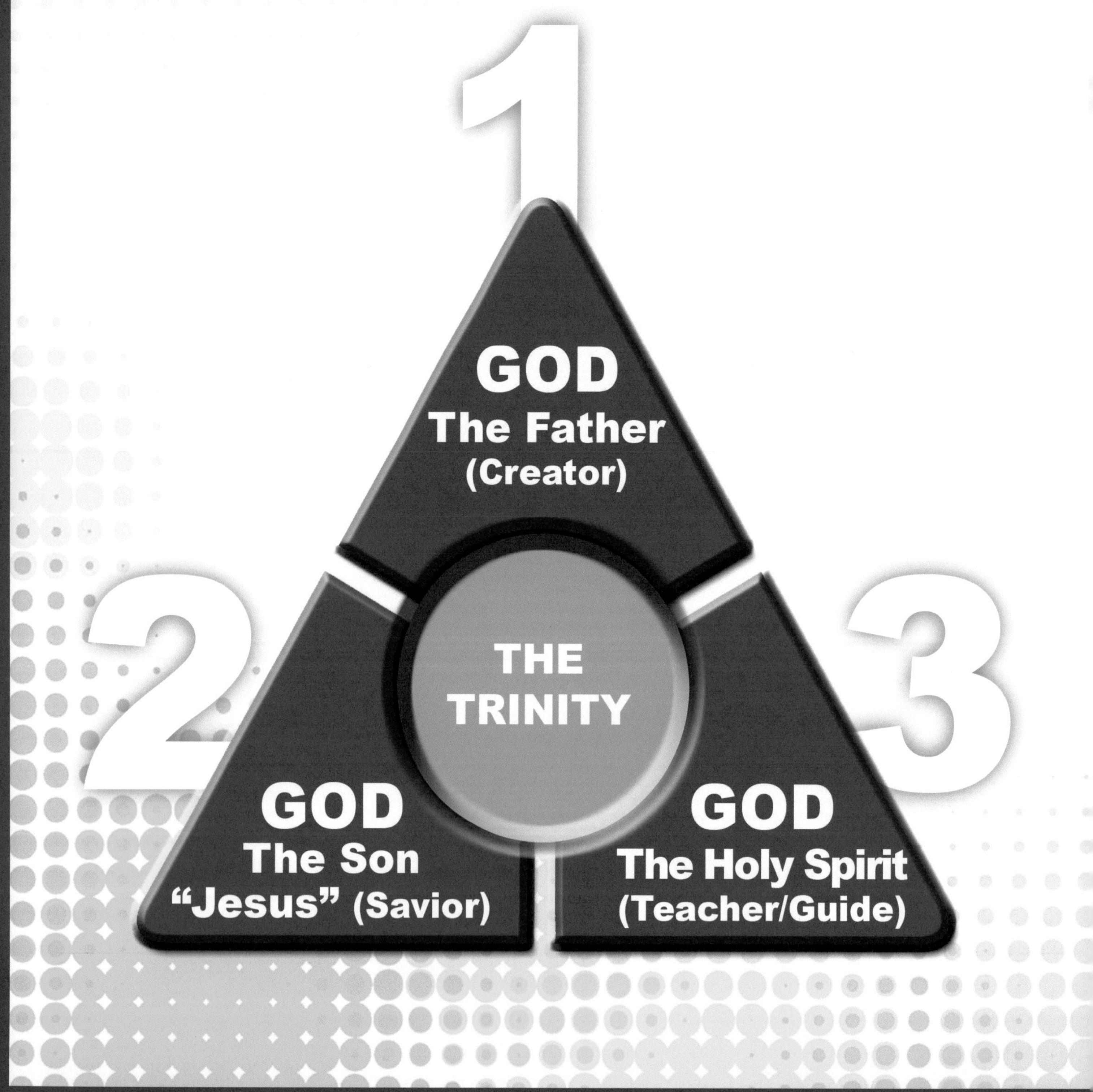
1
2
3
GOD
The Father
(Creator)
THE
TRINITY
GOD
The Son
“Jesus” (Savior)
GOD
The Holy Spirit
(Teacher/Guide)

A triangle has 3 sides. A triangle has 3 angles.

God works in 3 persons. This is called the Trinity. Let's use the triangle to understand the Trinity... the 3 persons of God.

The Father
(Creator)

The first person of God is The Father.

1 Light and Darkness
2 Sky and Water
3 Plants and Land
4 Stars, Moon and Sun
5 Flying Animals and Sea Life
6 Land Animals and People

In the beginning, there was God (Genesis 1). God has always been here. He is not human like us. He doesn't have a mom or dad. God is a spirit. He is eternal. This means that God will never go away. He has always been here and He will always be here.

God is our Father because He is the Creator. He created the universe and all of the planets. He created the sun, moon, stars, sky, day, night, the plants, birds, insects, animals, and His most important creation...PEOPLE!

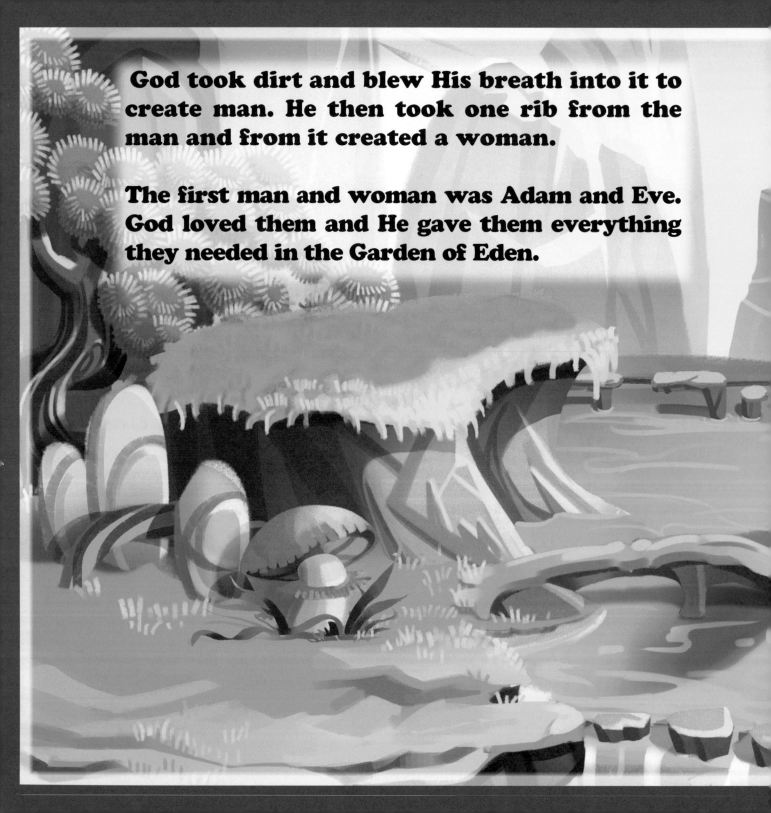

God took dirt and blew His breath into it to create man. He then took one rib from the man and from it created a woman.

The first man and woman was Adam and Eve. God loved them and He gave them everything they needed in the Garden of Eden.

God did not want people to love Him like robots. He wanted real love made by a choice. So, He gave Adam and Eve the ability to choose.

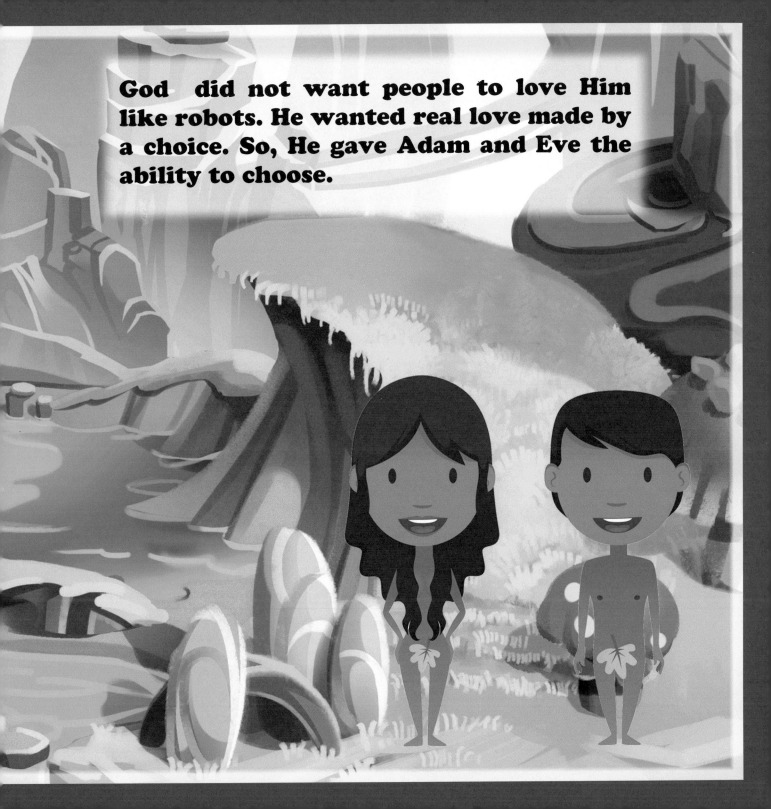

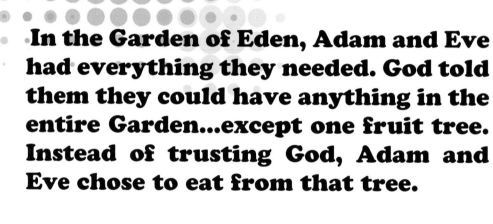

In the Garden of Eden, Adam and Eve had everything they needed. God told them they could have anything in the entire Garden...except one fruit tree. Instead of trusting God, Adam and Eve chose to eat from that tree.

This is how sin entered the world. Sin is anything that is done, said, or thought that goes against the knowledge of God.

God hates sin. He can't be around it. He can't look at it. Now that sin is in the world, God was blocked from people.

GOD
The Father
(Creator)

None of the people were able to help us get back to God. We needed a savior!

Jesus was born, just like you. The difference is, God is His Father. Jesus never sinned.

He went to church and grew up to learn all about what God wanted him to do. He lived to show us how to live.

He then took the punishment for all of our sins and died on the cross so that we can have a relationship with God.

Jesus died on the cross for you! He was buried in a tomb and stayed there for three days. His death was only for a moment. Since He is God, He rose from the dead. Now, He talks to God about you, and what you ask from God. Everyone who believes in Jesus is saved and has a place in heaven!

GOD
The Father
(Creator)

GOD
The Son
"Jesus" (Savior)

God loved us so much that He sent His only begotten Son, Jesus! He would take the punishment for our sins. Jesus didn't come to tell us how bad we are. He came to save us!
(John 3:16-17)

Jesus is the Son of God. He saved me. He wants to save you, too. Just say out loud...
* I believe Jesus Christ is the Son of God.
* I believe Jesus Christ died on the cross for my sins.
* I believe Jesus Christ rose from the dead.
* I want Jesus Christ to live in my heart.

YAY! YOU SAID IT! Now you are saved and the Holy Spirit lives in your heart.

Holy Spirit says this way

Now, the third person of God is always with you.
The third person of God is the Holy Spirit.

The Holy Spirit is the Spirit of God who lives inside of you. He is your teacher and your guide. He speaks to you and tells you what God wants you to do. You hear from the Holy Spirit when you:

* Read and study the Bible
* Go to church and worship God
* Listen to your pastor and church school teacher
* Are obedient to God and you do what He asks of you.

1
2
3
GOD
The Father
(Creator)
THE
TRINITY
GOD
The Son
“Jesus” (Savior)
GOD
The Holy Spirit
(Teacher/Guide)

Now you understand the Trinity.

Remember to read the
Bible every day.

God has special plans for you.
Grow closer to Him and He will direct
your whole life (Jeremiah 29:11).

About my spiritual journey

Name:_____

Age:_____

Birthday:_____

Baptized on:_____

Church:_____

Pastor:_____

Who came to see me get baptized:_____

_____

How I felt after I was baptized:_____

_____

_____

Dr. Betty D. Dennis is a minister-in-training at Mt. Zion Baptist Church in Kalamazoo, Michigan. She serves as a Christian educator and is dedicated to share Christ with youth. She was inspired to write this book for children when she realized the complexity of the Trinity and the need to shared it in a way children could understand.

Dr. Dennis is a faculty specialist for Western Michigan University's School of Interdisciplinary Health Programs. She received a Ph.D. in higher educational leadership in 2007. She and her husband, Tony, have three children.

This book is dedicated to my family. My husband Tony, our children Imani, Amyre, and Tony Jr.; my brother, Robert, and sister, Vanessa. Thank you for your love and support.

A special thank you to Pastor, Dr. Addis Moore, and Mt. Zion Baptist Church (Kalamazoo, Michigan). Thank you for helping me discover my purpose and continuously equipping me for the work of the ministry.

Published in collaboration with Fortitude Graphic Design and Printing and Season Press LLC
Artwork, Design and layout by Sean Hollins
Editing consultant Sonya Hollins

God in Three Persons: Understanding the Trinity/ Betty Dennis
p. cm.

ISBN: 978-0-9977136-8-8

1. Religion—Trinity. 2. Biblical–Education. 3. Youth
First Edition

10 9 8 7 6 5 4 3 2 1

Printed in the United States of America

Made in the USA
Columbia, SC
15 January 2024

30507160R00018